USING DIGITAL TECHNOLOGY

Steffi Cavell-Clarke & Thomas Welch

COMPUTERS
AND
<CODING>

©2018
Book Life
King's Lynn
Norfolk PE30 4LS

ISBN: 978-1-78637-278-9

Written by:
Steffi Cavell-Clarke & Thomas Welch

Edited by:
Kirsty Holmes

Designed by:
Danielle Jones

A catalogue record for this book
is available from the British Library

IMAGE CREDITS

Cover – izabel.l, I000s_pixels, Macrovector, danjazzia. 4 – vladwel, peiyang. 5 – Sudowoodo , Inspiring, Oceans, johavel. 6 – Art Alex, Inspiring, Jane Kelly, Sudowoodo. 7 – Lightkite. 8 – vladwel, Dim Tik. 10 – vladwel, peiyang. 11 – ,I000s_pixels, Sudowoodo. 12-13 – Sudowoodo. 14 – Ksiy1996, Holla Wise, Julia Tim. 15 – Sudowoodo, Jane Kelly. 16 – Lightkite, Marketa Kuchynkova, Nazarkru, Antonio Francois, o_du_van. 17 – Paul Lesser, T. Lesia, Brilliantist Studio, Evgeniya Mukhitova, mrwebhoney, Antonio Francois. 18 – Sudowoodo. 19 – Sudowoodo, Kit8.net, HieroGraphic. 20 – Trifonenkolvan. 21 – Sudowoodo, Art Alex, Trifonenkolvan. 22 – Sudowoodo, Thirap8l,   I000s_pixels. 23 – Dinosoft Labs, Sudowoodo.

Images are courtesy of Shutterstock.com. With thanks to Getty Images, Thinkstock Photo and iStockphoto.

All facts, statistics, web addresses and URLs in this book were verified as valid and accurate at time of writing. No responsibility for any changes to external websites or references can be accepted by either the author or publisher.

USING DIGITAL TECHNOLOGY

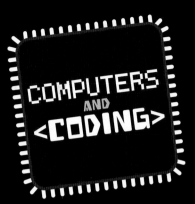

COMPUTERS AND <CODING>

Words that look like **this** can be found in the glossary on page 24.

WHAT IS DIGITAL TECHNOLOGY?

Digital technology is a term we use to describe **devices** and **systems** that store and use information electronically.

DIGITAL MEANS:

information or instructions stored in a computer language called code, using the **digits** 1 and 0.

TECHNOLOGY MEANS:

devices or tools that help us to do a job.

Digital technology is all around us and it comes in many different shapes and sizes.

Desktop Computer

Tablet

Smartphone

Laptop

DID YOU KNOW?
Online games, online shopping and **social media** are also digital technologies.

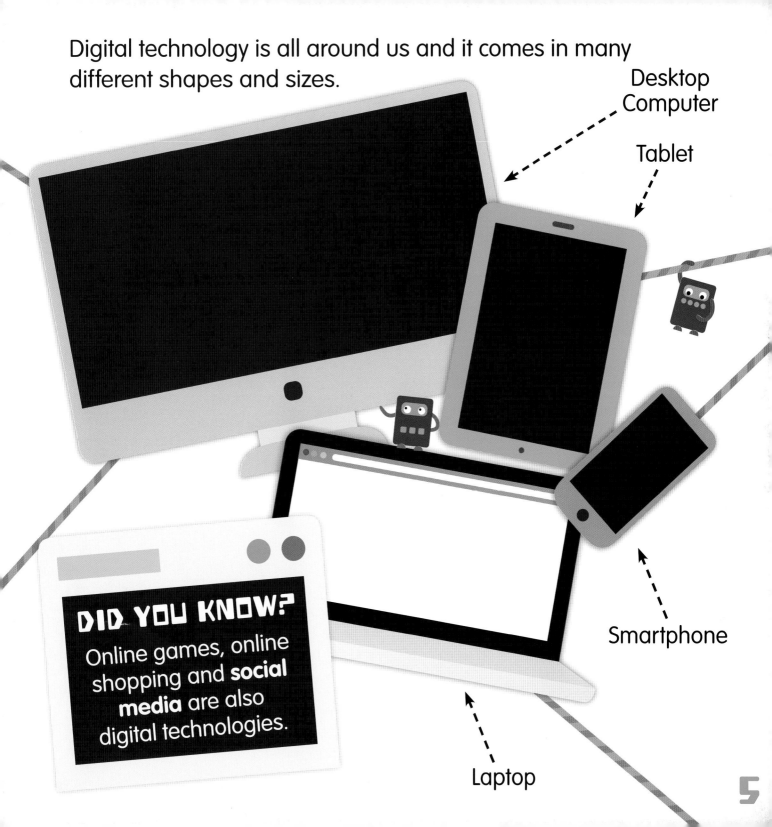

WHY IS DIGITAL TECHNOLOGY
IMPORTANT?

Digital technology has changed the way many people around the world **communicate**, learn and work.

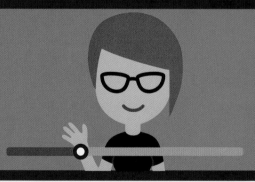

Digital technology shapes our lives every day. Whether we're working, playing or just talking to each other, we are likely to be using digital technology to help us.

DID YOU KNOW?

Digital technologies can store huge amounts of information on very small devices.

USING COMPUTERS

Digital technology uses computers to do things. Computers cannot think for themselves, so they need instructions to tell them what to do.

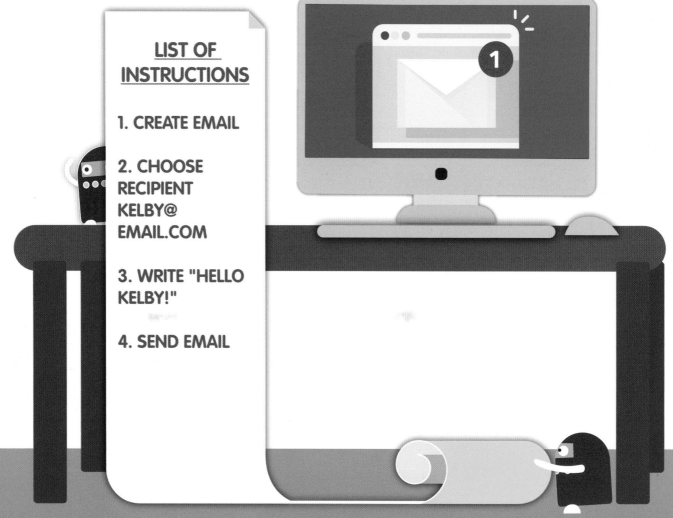

LIST OF INSTRUCTIONS

1. CREATE EMAIL

2. CHOOSE RECIPIENT KELBY@ EMAIL.COM

3. WRITE "HELLO KELBY!"

4. SEND EMAIL

A program is a list of instructions that tells a computer what to do. The list is known as an algorithm. It is written in a language that computers understand, called code.

```
>>>print('hello')
hello
```

USING THE
INTERNET

The Internet is a **network** of lots of computers that are linked together. This means that people from all over the world can communicate with each other.

You can use the Internet on computers, tablets and smartphones. The Internet can help you to do lots of things, such as talking to friends and family who live far away.

LAPTOPS AND TABLETS

Laptops are computers that can be easily carried around. Laptops can be used to do many tasks at once, like playing a game at the same time as watching a video.

A tablet is also a computer that can be carried around. You can use a tablet to take pictures, make videos, play games and use the Internet.

DID YOU KNOW?

Tablets use a touch-sensitive screen instead of a keyboard.

MOBILE PHONES

A mobile phone is a small, **wireless** device that can be held in your hand. Mobile phones are used to make calls and send text messages to other devices.

Mobile phones are just like any other computer and they can run lots of different types of programs. These programs are usually called apps.

DID YOU KNOW?
Phones that can run lots of different programs, just like a computer, are called smartphones.

SOCIAL MEDIA

Many people use digital technology to visit social media sites. These sites allow them to share information such as pictures, stories and videos.

People use social media to communicate with other people from all around the world.

REMEMBER

Never go alone to meet someone you have met online. If you really want to meet them, always take a parent or caregiver with you and go to a safe place where there are other people.

You should always be careful when **posting** anything online.

ONLINE GAMES

Many adults and children enjoy playing games online. They can use desktops, laptops, mobile phones, tablets and game consoles to play thousands of different games.

DID YOU KNOW?

Over 1.5 billion people around the world play computer games.

Online gaming means you can play with people from all around the world, but not everyone online is who they say they are. You shouldn't connect with people you do not know.

DIGITAL FOOTPRINT

Everyone who uses the Internet has a digital footprint.
This is the information they share about themselves online.

Every time we post a photo or a video, it adds to our digital footprint. Once something is stored on the Internet, it may be impossible to delete.

DIGITAL SECURITY

Digital technology can store a lot of **private information**. Always protect your technology using passwords and don't leave any devices for other people to find.

Digital technology is a big part of our lives, and it is changing every day. Who knows what amazing digital technology is coming in the future?

REMEMBER
Always let a **responsible** adult know when you are online.

GLOSSARY

COMMUNICATE	to pass information between two or more people
DEVICES	objects designed for a particular purpose, usually machines
DIGITS	any number between 0 and 9
NETWORK	a system of connected people or things
POSTING	uploading something online
PRIVATE INFORMATION	information, such as your name, address, school and what you look like, that tells other people who you are and where to find you
RESPONSIBLE	to be trusted to do the right thing
SOCIAL MEDIA	websites that let users create and share content with other people
SYSTEMS	sets of things that work together
WEBSITES	pages of information on the Internet
WIRELESS	a device that doesn't need to be plugged in

INDEX